This book belongs to

. . . .

It's fun to learn languages.

English
Thai
Japanese
Chinese

Please call me
in Japanese

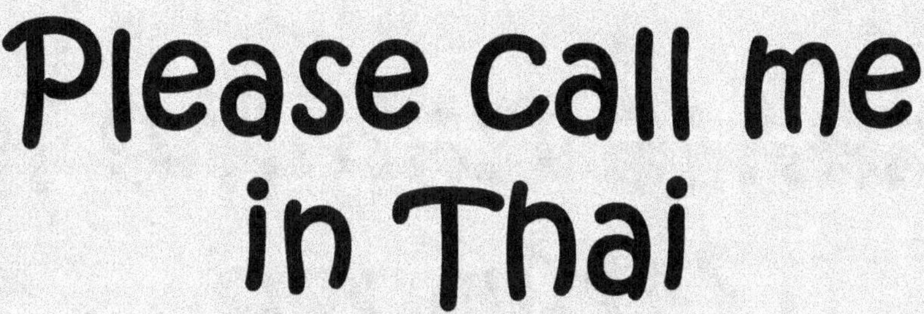

Please call me
in Thai

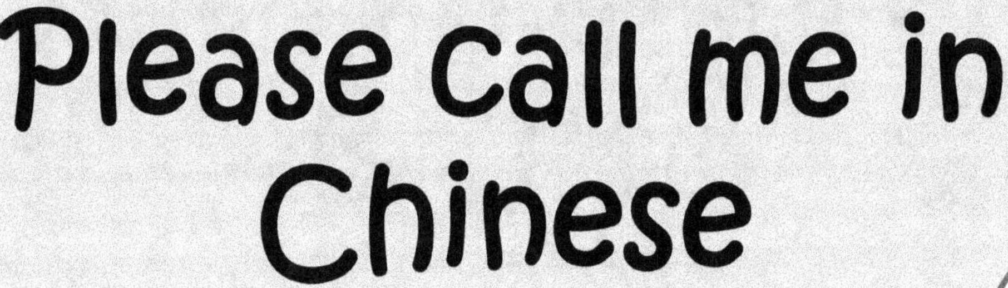
Please call me in
Chinese

Enjoy
Matching

English	frog	fräg,frôg
Japanese	カエル	Kaeru
Chinese	青蛙	Qīngwā
Thai	กบ	Kb

Let's have fun

English	dinosaur	dáynəsɔ̀r
Japanese	恐竜 (きょうりゅう)	Kyōryū
Chinese	恐龍	Kǒnglóng
Thai	ไดโนเสาร์	Dịnos̄eāŕ

English		
Japanese		
Chinese		
Thai		

English	Chameleon	čəmɛ́liən
Japanese	カメレオン	Kamereon
Chinese	變色龍	Biànsèlóng
Thai	กิ้งก่า	Kîngkā

English		
Japanese		
Chinese		
Thai		

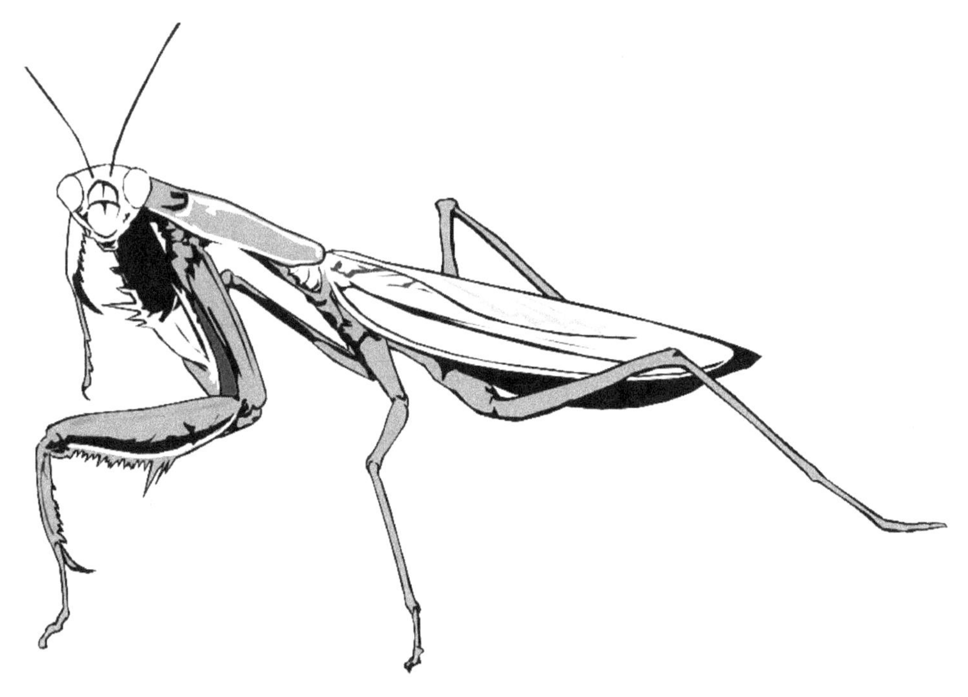

English	mantis	mǽntìs
Japanese	カマキリ	Kamakiri
Chinese	螳螂	Tángláng
Thai	ตั๊กแตนตำข้าว	Táktæn tảm kȳĥāw

English		
Japanese		
Chinese		
Thai		

English	firefly	fáyərflày
Japanese	ホタル	Hotaru
Chinese	螢火蟲	Yínghuǒ chóng
Thai	หิ่งห้อย	H̄ìngĥxy

English		
Japanese		
Chinese		
Thai		

English	ladybug	ˈlādēbəg
Japanese	てんとう虫	Tentōchū
Chinese	瓢蟲	Piáo chóng
Thai	เต่าทอง	Tèāthxng

English		
Japanese		
Chinese		
Thai		

Call them in Japanese
Matching

Kyōryū

Kamereon

Tentōchū

Kamakiri

Hotaru

Call them in Japanese
Matching

Kyōryū

Kamereon

Tentōchū

Kamakiri

Hotaru

Call them in Chinese
Matching

Biànsèlóng

Piáo chóng

Kǒnglóng

Tángláng

Yínghuǒ chóng

Call them in Chinese
Matching

Biànsèlóng
Piáo chóng
Kǒnglóng
Tángláng
Yínghuǒ chóng

Call them in Thai
Matching

Kîngkā

Hìngĥxy

Dịnōsĕāŕ

Tèāthxng

Tặktæn tảm k̄hāw

Call them in Thai
Matching

Kîngkā
Hìngĥxy
Dịnoŝeāŕ
Tèāthxng
Tặktæn tảm kĥāw

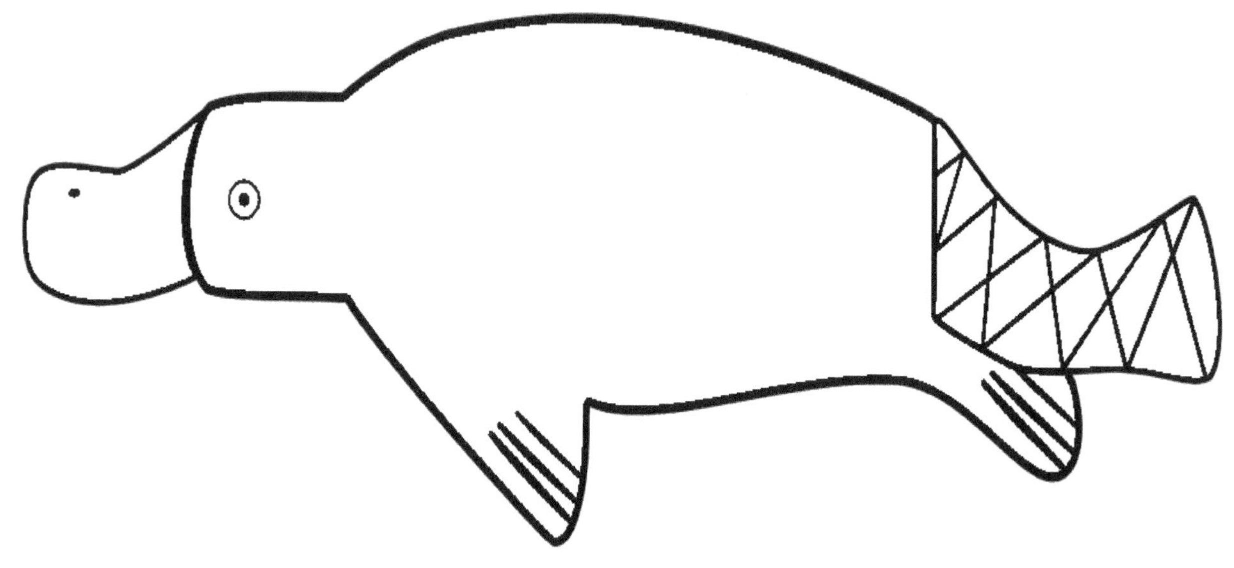

English	Platypus	ˈplatəpəs
Japanese	カモノハシ	Kamonoha shi
Chinese	鴨嘴獸	Yāzuǐshòu
Thai	ตุ่นปากเป็ด	Tùn pākpĕd

English		
Japanese		
Chinese		
Thai		

English	Bison	ˈbīsən
Japanese	バイソン	Baison
Chinese	野牛	Yěniú
Thai	วัวกระทิง	Wạw krathing

English		
Japanese		
Chinese		
Thai		

English	mosquito	məskíto
Japanese	蚊	Ka
Chinese	蚊子	Wénzi
Thai	ยุง	Yung

English		
Japanese		
Chinese		
Thai		

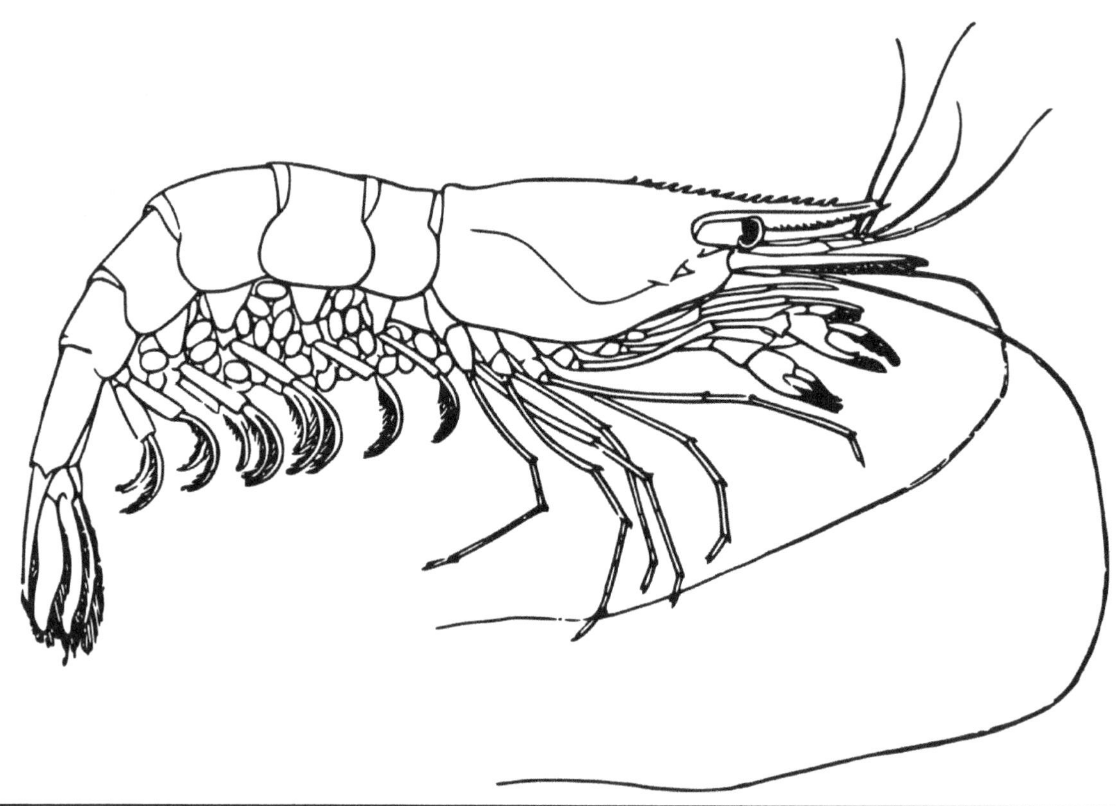

English	shrimp	šrímp
Japanese	エビ	Ebi
Chinese	鮮蝦	Xiān xiā
Thai	กุ้ง	Kûng

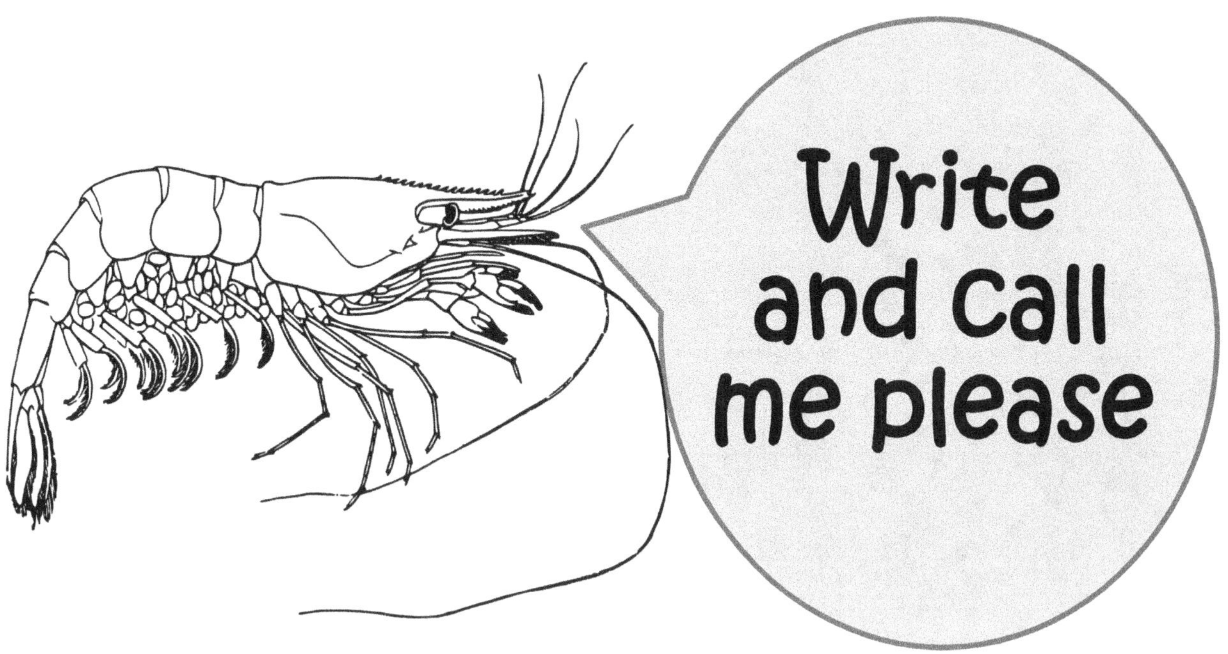

English		
Japanese		
Chinese		
Thai		

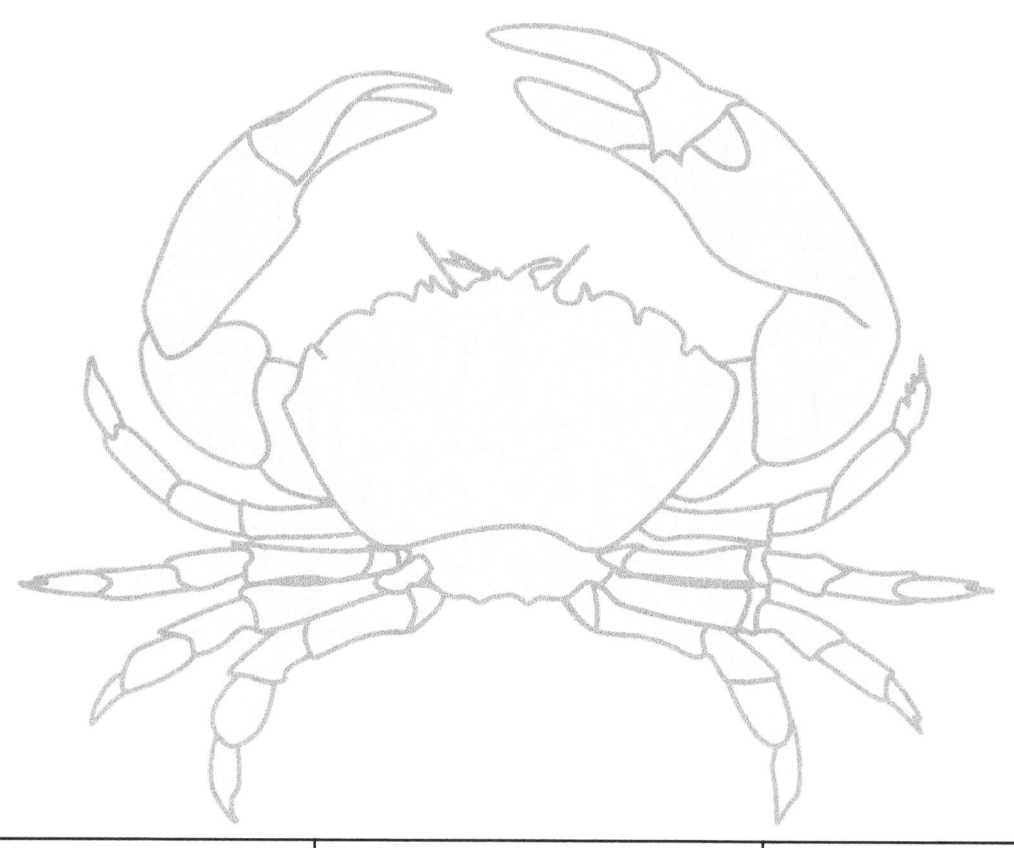

English	crab	krab
Japanese	カニ	Kani
Chinese	螃蟹	Pángxiè
Thai	ปู	Pū

English		
Japanese		
Chinese		
Thai		

English	goose	gús
Japanese	ガチョウ	Gachō
Chinese	鵝	É
Thai	ห่าน	Ȟān

English		
Japanese		
Chinese		
Thai		

Call them in Japanese Matching

| Ebi |
| Kamonohashi |
| Ka |
| Baison |
| Gachō |
| Kani |

Call them in Japanese Matching

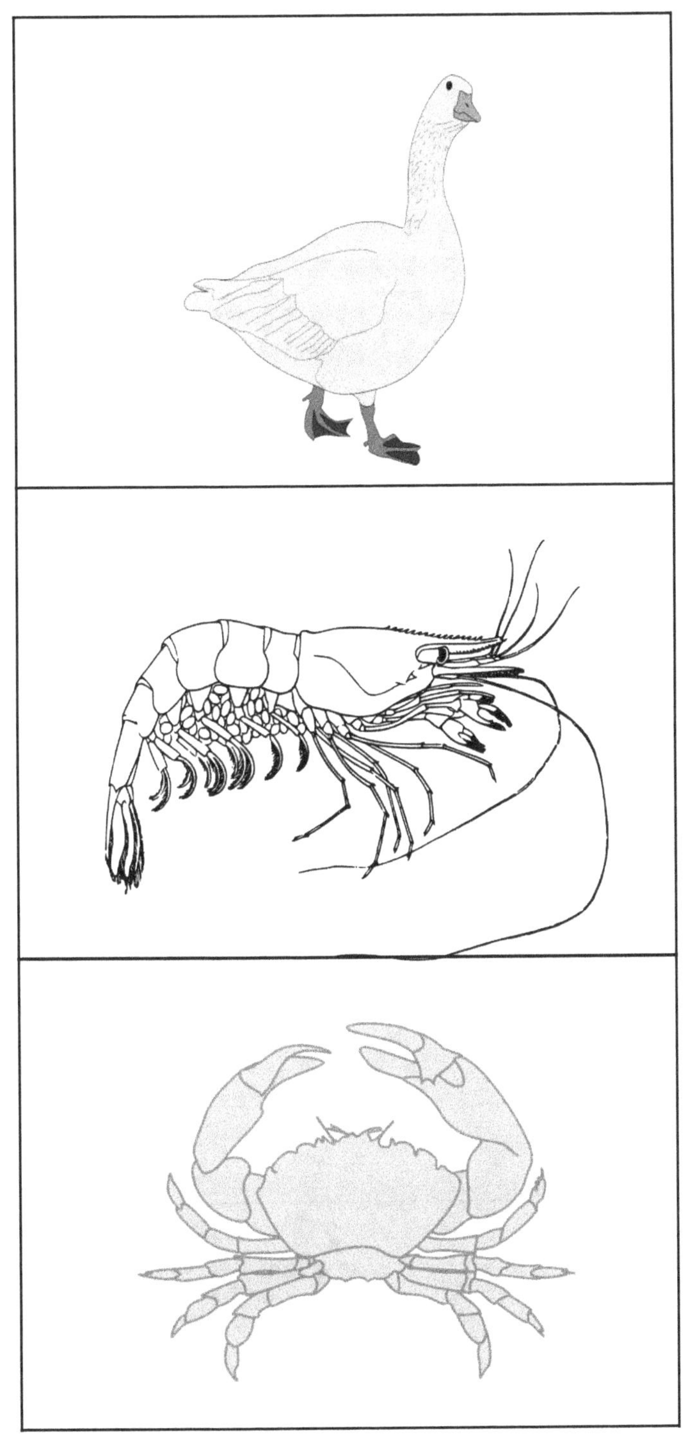

Ebi
Kamonohashi
Ka
Baison
Gachō
Kani

Call them in Chinese
Matching

| Wénzi |
| Yāzuǐshòu |
| Pángxiè |
| É |
| Xiān xiā |
| Yěniú |

Call them in Chinese
Matching

Wénzi
Yāzuǐshòu
Pángxiè
É
Xiān xiā
Yěniú

Call them in Thai
Matching

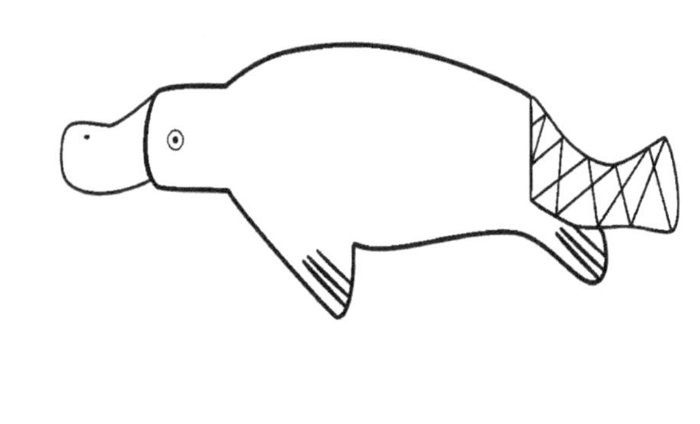

Wạw krathing
Yung
Kûng
H̀ān
Pū
Tùn pākpĕd

Call them in Thai
Matching

Wạw krathing
Yung
Kûng
H̀ān
Pū
Tùn pākpĕd

English	weasel	wízəl
Japanese	イタチ	Itachi
Chinese	黃鼠狼	Huángshǔláng
Thai	พังพอน	Phạngphxn

English		
Japanese		
Chinese		
Thai		

English	sea horse	sí hórs
Japanese	タツノオトシゴ	Tatsunōtoshigo
Chinese	海馬	Hǎimǎ
Thai	ม้าน้ำ	M̂ān̂am

English		
Japanese		
Chinese		
Thai		

English	spider	spáydər
Japanese	クモ	Kumo
Chinese	隻蜘蛛	zhī zhīzhū
Thai	แมงมุม	Mængmum

English		
Japanese		
Chinese		
Thai		

English	sea lion	sí láyən
Japanese	アシカ	Ashika
Chinese	海獅	Hǎishī
Thai	สิงโตทะเล	Ŝingtothale

English		
Japanese		
Chinese		
Thai		

English	antelope	ǽntəlòp
Japanese	アンテ ロープ	Anterōpu
Chinese	羚羊	Língyáng
Thai	ละมั่ง	La mạng

English		
Japanese		
Chinese		
Thai		

English	Oysters	ɔ̀ystərz
Japanese	カキ	Kaki
Chinese	牡蠣	Mǔlì
Thai	หอยนางรม	Ĥxy nāngrm

English		
Japanese		
Chinese		
Thai		

Call them in Japanese
Matching

Anterōpu
Kaki
Tatsunōtoshigo
Ashika
Itachi
Kumo

Call them in Japanese Matching

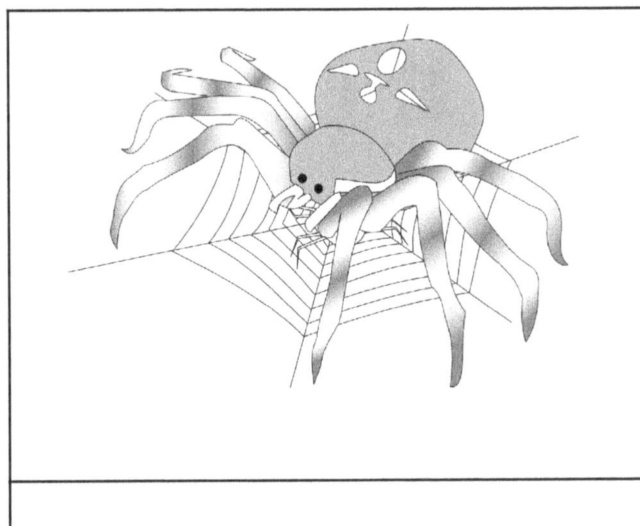

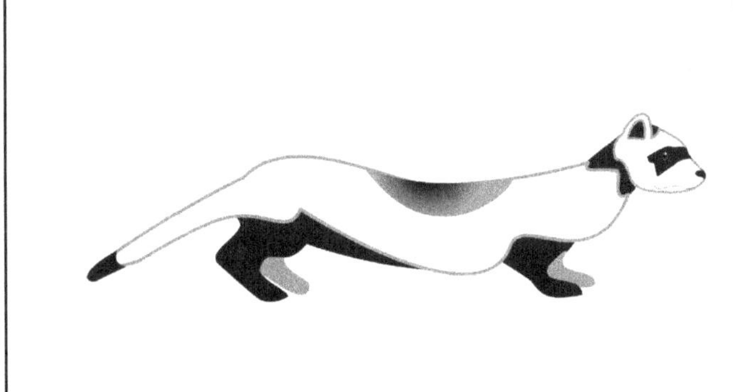

Anterōpu
Kaki
Tatsunōtoshigo
Ashika
Itachi
Kumo

Call them in Chinese Matching

zhī zhīzhū
Huángshǔláng
Mǔlì
Hǎishī
Língyáng
Hǎimǎ

Call them in Chinese
Matching

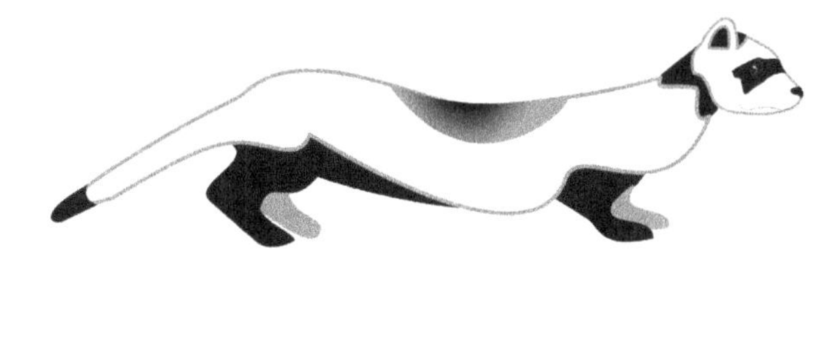

zhī zhīzhū
Huángshǔláng
Mǔlì
Hǎishī
Língyáng
Hǎimǎ

Call them in Thai
Matching

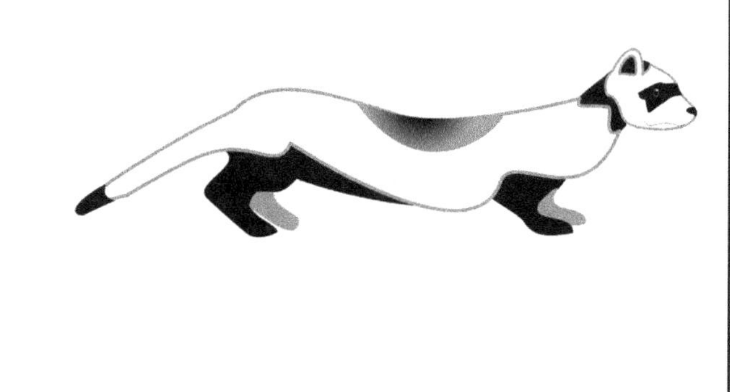

Mængmum
Ħxy nāngrm
Šingtothale
Phạngphxn
La mạng
M̂āñam

Call them in Thai
Matching

Mængmum
Ḥxy nāngrm
Ṣ̄ingtothale
Phạngphxn
La màng
M̂ā̂nam

English	penguin	péŋgwən
Japanese	ペンギン	Pengin
Chinese	企鵝	Qì'é
Thai	เพนกวิน	Phenkwin

English		
Japanese		
Chinese		
Thai		

English	hawk, falcon	Hôk, fǽlkən
Japanese	ホーク	Hōku
Chinese	鷹派	Yīngpài
Thai	เหยี่ยว	Ḥeyìyw

English		
Japanese		
Chinese		
Thai		

English	camel	ˈkaməl
Japanese	ラクダ	Rakuda
Chinese	駱駝	Luòtuó
Thai	อูฐ	Xūṭh

English		
Japanese		
Chinese		
Thai		

English	calf	kaf
Japanese	ゾウの赤ちゃん	Zō no akachan
Chinese	小象	Xiǎo xiàng
Thai	ลูกช้าง	Lūkchâng

English		
Japanese		
Chinese		
Thai		

English	giraffe	jəˈraf
Japanese	キリン	Kirin
Chinese	長頸鹿	Chángjǐnglù
Thai	ยีราฟ	Yīrāf

English		
Japanese		
Chinese		
Thai		

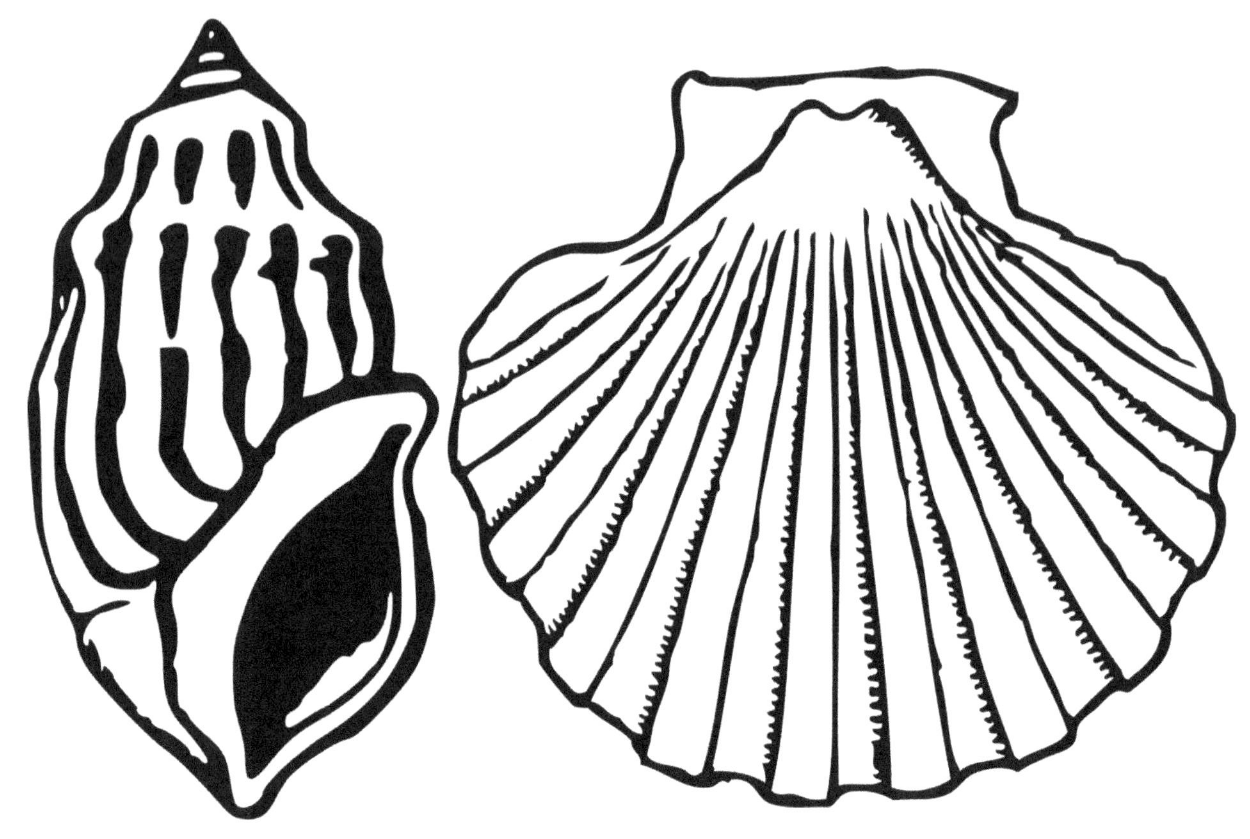

English	shellfish	šɛ́lfìš
Japanese	シェル	Sheru
Chinese	砲彈	Pàodàn
Thai	หอย	Ḥxy

English		
Japanese		
Chinese		
Thai		

Call them in Japanese
Matching

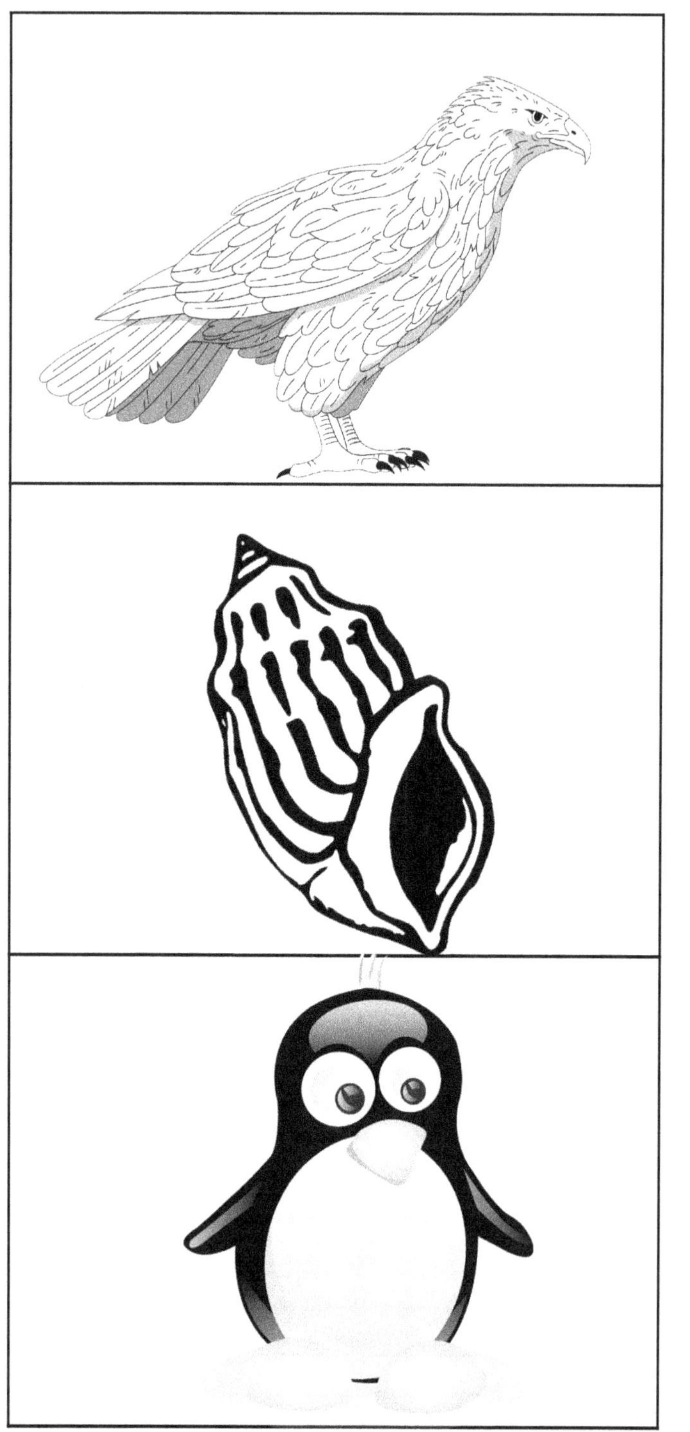

Kirin
Rakuda
Zō no akachan
Pengin
Sheru
Hōku

Call them in Japanese
Matching

Kirin

Rakuda

Zō no akachan

Pengin

Sheru

Hōku

Call them in Chinese
Matching

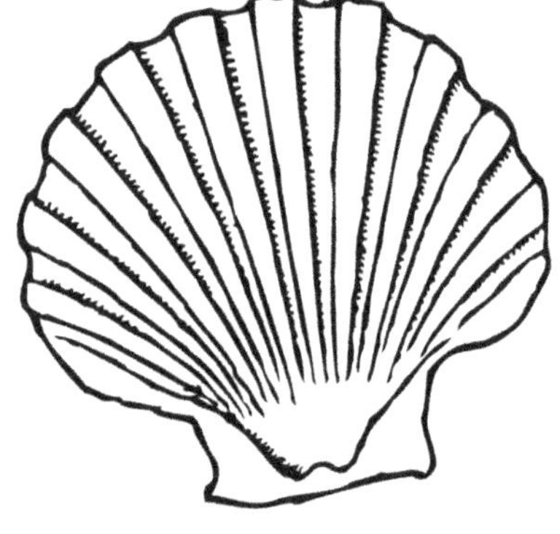

Luòtuó
Qì'é
Chángjǐnglù
Yīngpài
Pàodàn
Xiǎo xiàng

Call them in Chinese
Matching

Luòtuó
Qì'é
Chángjǐnglù
Yīngpài
Pàodàn
Xiǎo xiàng

Call them in Thai
Matching

Ḡeyìyw
Xūṭh
Lūkcĥāng
Yīrāf
Ḡxy
Phenkwin

Call them in Thai
Matching

Ēeyỳyw
Xūṭh
Lūkchâng
Yīrāf
Ḥxy
Phenkwin

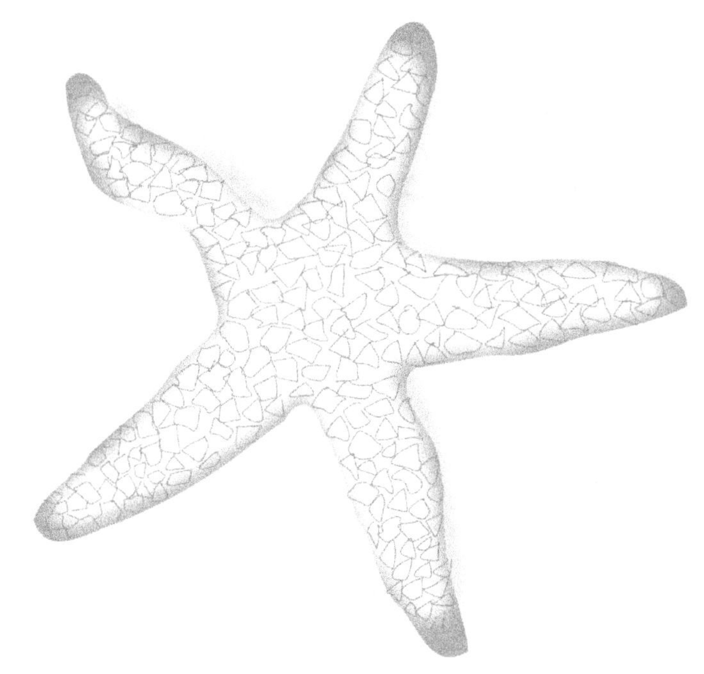

English	starfish	stárfìš
Japanese	ヒトデ	Hitode
Chinese	海星	Hǎixīng
Thai	ปลาดาว	Plādāw

English		
Japanese		
Chinese		
Thai		

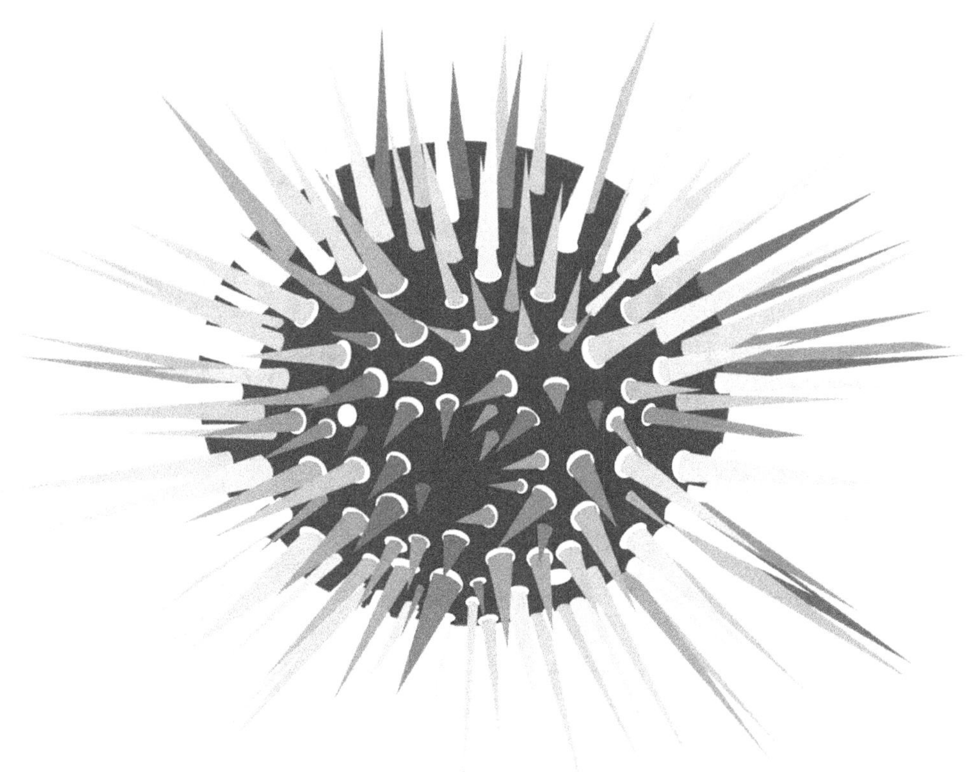

English	Sea urchin	sí ə́rčən
Japanese	ウニ	Uni
Chinese	海膽	Hǎi dǎn
Thai	เม่นทะเล	Mènthale

English		
Japanese		
Chinese		
Thai		

English	fish	fìš
Japanese	魚	Sakana
Chinese	條魚	Tiáo yú
Thai	ปลา	Plā

English		
Japanese		
Chinese		
Thai		

English	Jellyfish	jĕlifìš
Japanese	クラゲ	Kurage
Chinese	海蜇	Hǎizhē
Thai	แมงกระพรุน	Mæng kra phrun

English		
Japanese		
Chinese		
Thai		

English	Puffer fish	pə́fər fíš
Japanese	フグ	Fugu
Chinese	河豚	Hétún
Thai	ปลาปักเป้า	Plā pa̱kpêā

English		
Japanese		
Chinese		
Thai		

English	góldfish	góldfìš
Japanese	金魚	Kingyo
Chinese	金魚	Jīnyú
Thai	ปลาทอง	Plāthxng

English		
Japanese		
Chinese		
Thai		

Call them in Japanese
Matching

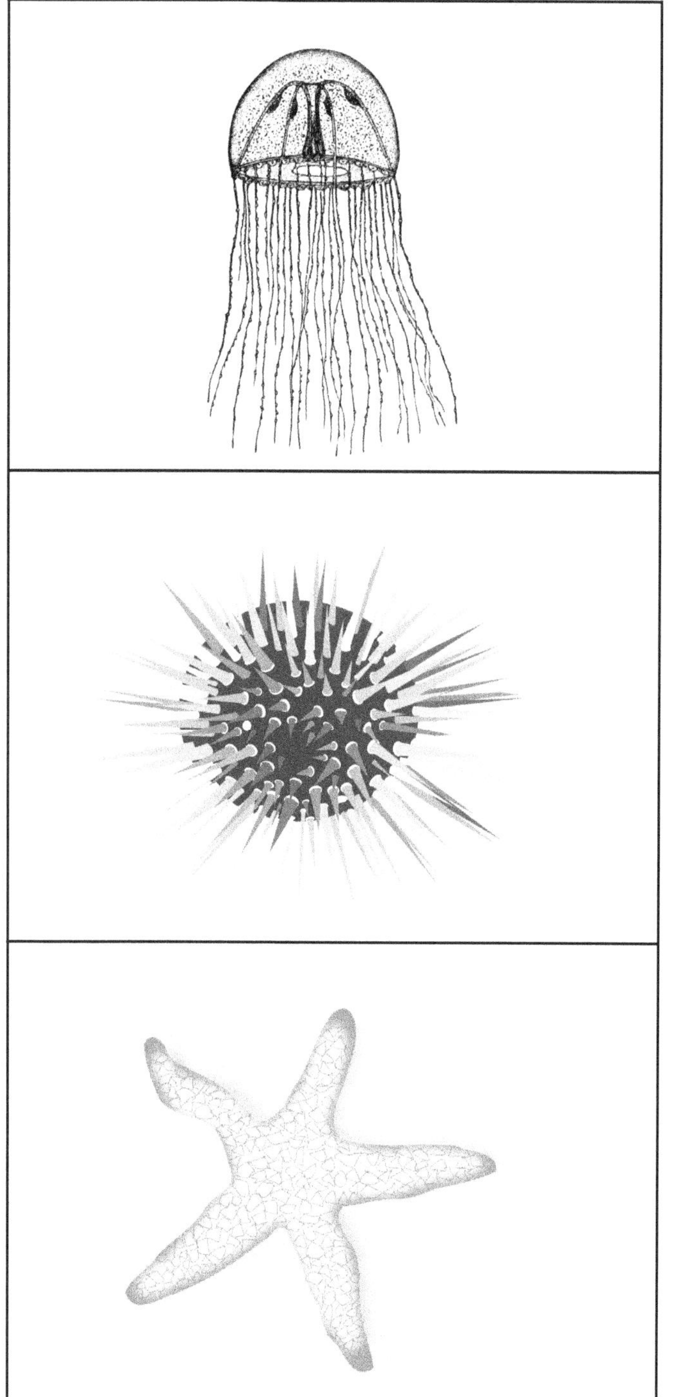

Kurage
Kingyo
Uni
Hitode
Sakana
Fugu

Call them in Japanese Matching

Kurage
Kingyo
Uni
Hitode
Sakana
Fugu

Call them in Chinese
Matching

Tiáo yú
Hǎixīng
Hétún
Jīnyú
Hǎizhē
Hǎi dǎn

Call them in Chinese
Matching

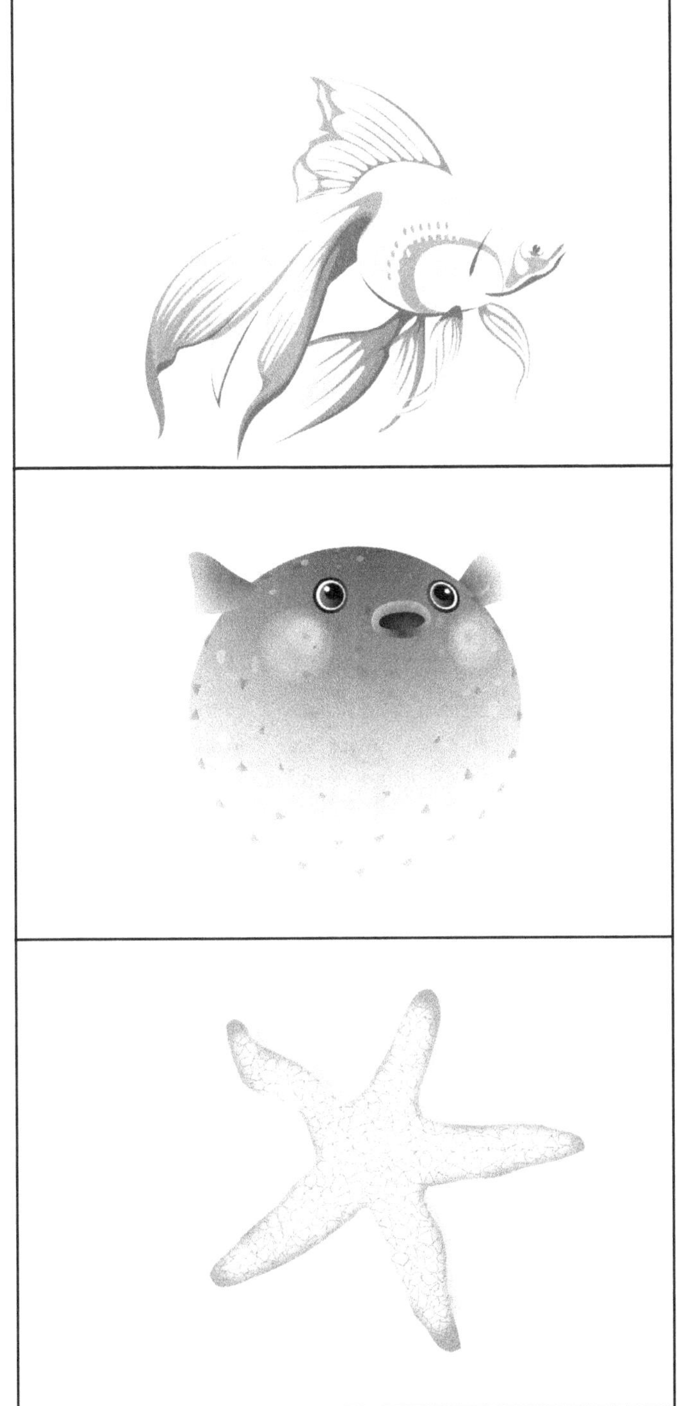

Tiáo yú
Hǎixīng
Hétún
Jīnyú
Hǎizhē
Hǎi dǎn

Call them in Thai
Matching

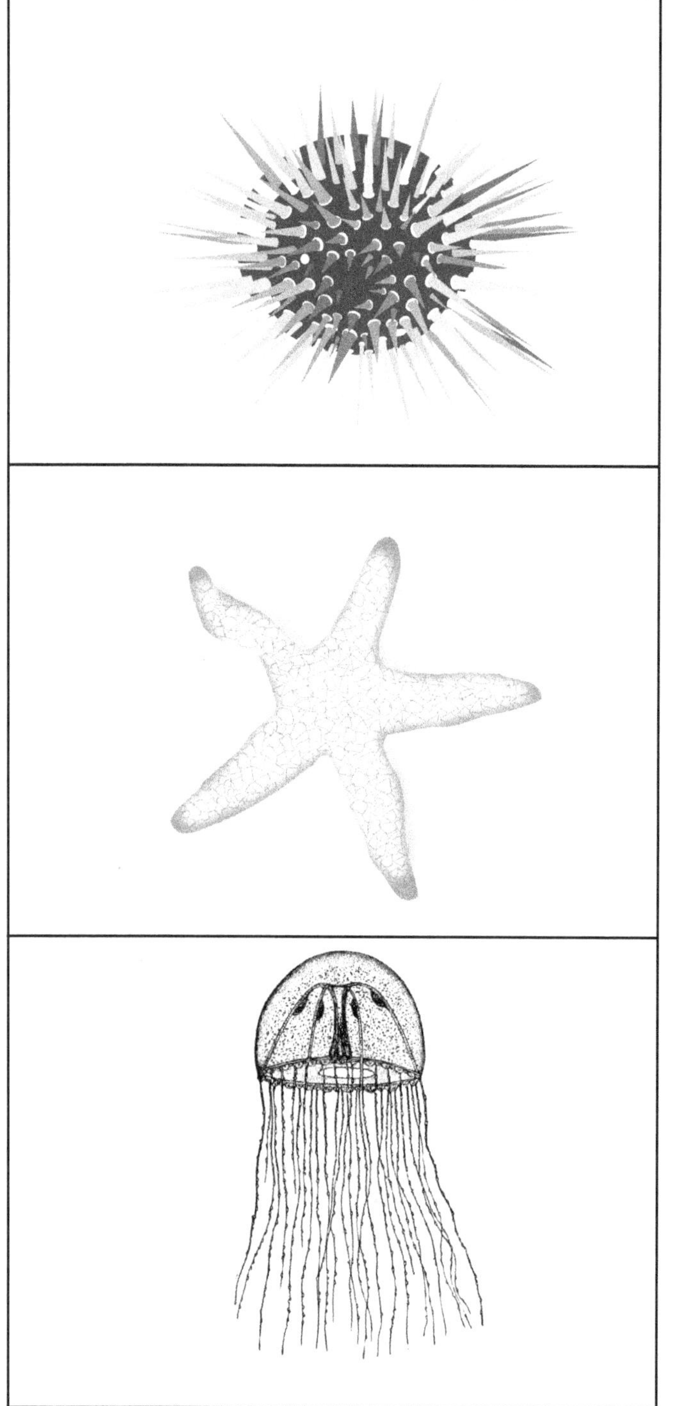

Plā
Mæng kra phrun
Plāthxng
Plādāw
Plā pa̧kpêā
Mènthale

Call them in Thai
Matching

Plā
Mæng kra phrun
Plāthxng
Plādāw
Plā pạkpêā
Mènthale

SUPER

4

Lang

Fun

English	
Japanese	
Chinese	
Thai	

English	
Japanese	
Chinese	
Thai	

English	
Japanese	
Chinese	
Thai	

English	
Japanese	
Chinese	
Thai	

English	
Japanese	
Chinese	
Thai	

English	
Japanese	
Chinese	
Thai	

English	
Japanese	
Chinese	
Thai	

English	
Japanese	
Chinese	
Thai	

English	
Japanese	
Chinese	
Thai	

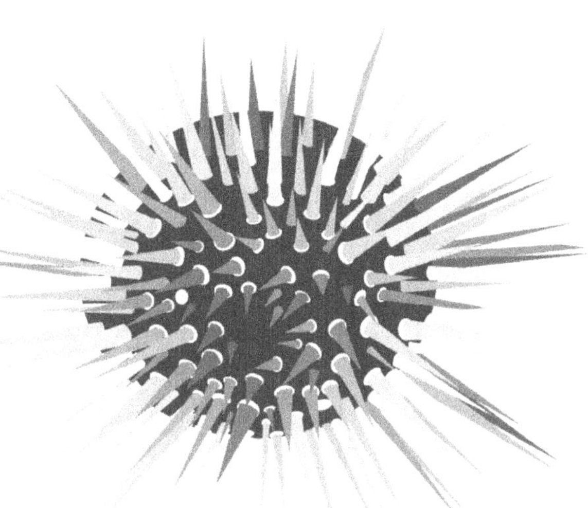

English	
Japanese	
Chinese	
Thai	

English	
Japanese	
Chinese	
Thai	

English	
Japanese	
Chinese	
Thai	

English	
Japanese	
Chinese	
Thai	

English	
Japanese	
Chinese	
Thai	

English	
Japanese	
Chinese	
Thai	

English	
Japanese	
Chinese	
Thai	

English	
Japanese	
Chinese	
Thai	

English	
Japanese	
Chinese	
Thai	

English	
Japanese	
Chinese	
Thai	

English	
Japanese	
Chinese	
Thai	

English	
Japanese	
Chinese	
Thai	

English	
Japanese	
Chinese	
Thai	

English	
Japanese	
Chinese	
Thai	

English	
Japanese	
Chinese	
Thai	

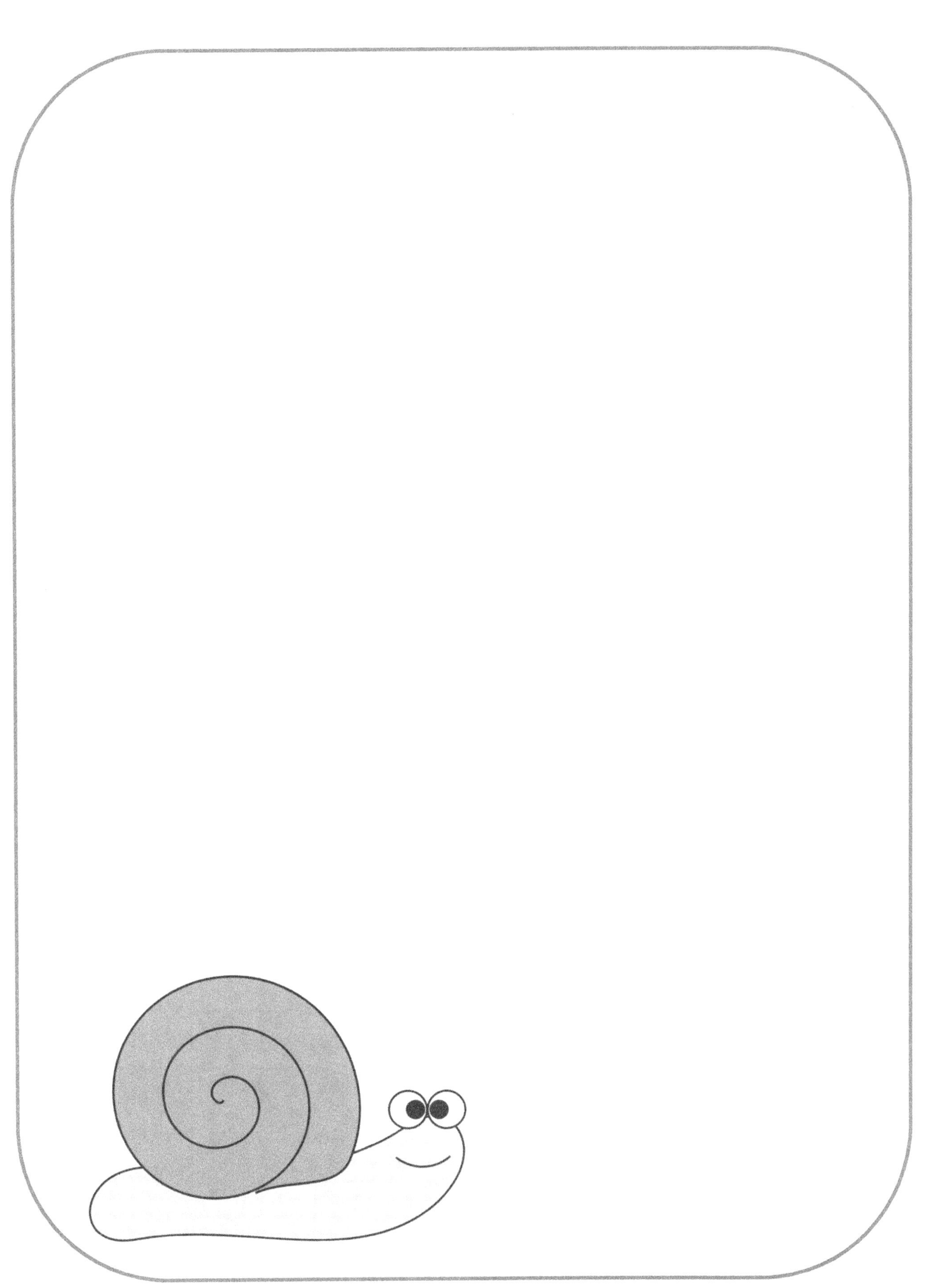

www.ingramcontent.com/pod-product-compliance
Lightning Source LLC
Chambersburg PA
CBHW060118120726
48003CB00009B/2694